PEOPLE AT THE CENTER OF

THE VIETNAM WAR

By ROB EDELMAN

BLACKBIRCH™
PRESS

THOMSON

GALE

San Diego • Detroit • New York • San Francisco • Cleveland
New Haven, Conn. • Waterville, Maine • London • Munich

For more information, contact
The Gale Group, Inc.
27500 Drake Rd.
Farmington Hills, MI 48331-3535
Or you can visit our Internet site at http://www.gale.com

Photo credits: cover, pages 4, 5, 6, 7, 9, 12, 14, 15, 20, 24, 26, 27, 31, 34, 37, 40, 41, 45 ©
Bettmann/CORBIS; pages 8, 29, 30, 39 © Wally McNamee/CORBIS; pages 10, 28 © Steve
Raymer/CORBIS; page 11 © Francooise de Mulder/CORBIS; page 13, 16 © CORBIS; pages 18, 22,
23 © AP Wide World; page 19 © Hulton/Archive; page 25 © Catherine Karnow/CORBIS; page
22 © Owen Franken/CORBIS; page 35, 42 © Reuters NewMedia Inc./CORBIS; page 36 © Joseph
Sohm; ChromoSohm Inc./CORBIS; page 43 © CORBIS SYGMA

LIBRARY OF CONGRESS CATALOGING-IN-PUBLICATION DATA

Edelman, Rob.
  The Vietnam War / by Rob Edelman.
    p. cm. — (People at the center of:)
  Summary: Profiles people involved in the Vietnam War as soldiers, politicians, or protest-
ers, including Lyndon Johnson, Ho Chi Minh, John McCain, and Abbie Hoffman.
  Includes bibliographical references and index.
  ISBN 1-56711-771-6 (hard : alk. paper)
  1. Vietnamese Conflict, 1961-1975—Biography—Juvenile literature. [1. Vietnamese
Conflict, 1961-1975—Biography.] I. Title. II. Series.

  DS557.5.E34 2004
  959.704'3'0922—dc21   2003008049

CONTENTS

THE VIETNAM WAR

Vietnam is a narrow, thousand-mile-long country located in the Southeastern part of Asia. It is bordered by three nations—China (directly to its north), Laos (northwest), and Cambodia (southwest)—as well as three bodies of water—the Gulf of Thailand (southwest), the South China Sea (southeast), and the Gulf of Tonkin (northeast).

Above: Japanese soldiers invaded Vietnam, which was then under French rule, in 1941 and occupied the country until the end of World War II. Opposite: The French fought and captured many Viet Minh fighters during the first Indochina War.

During the mid–twentieth century, Vietnam was the site of a brutal, controversial war. The roots of this conflict date to the mid–nineteenth century. In 1859, France seized control of Saigon, a major Vietnamese city, and took over the southern Cochin China region three years later.

The French remained in control until World War II (1939–1945), when the Japanese occupied Vietnam (then known as Indochina). In 1941, a year after the Japanese invaded the country, Ho Chi Minh—the most important figure in Vietnam during the twentieth century—established the Communist-dominated Vietnam Independence League (or Viet Minh) to battle the Japanese. On September 2, 1945, the day the Japanese surrendered to end the war, Ho read the Vietnamese Declaration of Independence to a gathering of five hundred thousand people in Hanoi, the North Vietnamese capital. The document was based on the U.S. Declaration of Independence and the French Declaration of the Rights of Man and the Citizen. The French, however, reestablished their power in the South and refused to grant the South Vietnamese people their freedom. From 1946 through 1954, Viet Minh fighters waged a war from the North against the French, and battled in the country's mountains and rice paddies. This come to be known as the first Indochina War.

After the French withdrew from Vietnam in 1954, world leaders met in Geneva, Switzerland, where they reached an agreement to temporarily divide Vietnam into the Communist North and non-Communist South.

In 1954, after their defeat at Dien Bien Phu, a northern military outpost, the French withdrew from Vietnam. Independence and peace, however, were not at hand. The same year, representatives of the United States, Soviet Union, Great Britain, China, and France met in Geneva, Switzerland, to determine the fate of Vietnam. They could not agree upon what that future would be so they temporarily divided Vietnam, at the 17th parallel, into two sections: the Communist North, which was ruled by Ho Chi Minh, and the U.S.-backed, non-Communist South. National elections that would unite North and South as one nation were scheduled for July, 1956.

During this period, the United States was involved in a Cold War (or nonshooting war) with the world's Communist nations, which stretched across the globe from East Germany to China to the Soviet Union. It was a struggle in which American democracy and free enterprise were pitted against the principle that a state-operated financial system is preferable to private ownership. While the Cold War was a conflict of beliefs, the threat of nuclear war, particularly against the Soviet Union, was ever present as both sides constructed and accumulated vast numbers of nuclear weapons.

Throughout the Cold War, the primary objective of U.S. foreign policy was to halt the spread of communism, which was viewed as a threat to democracy. To accomplish this goal, American policy makers deemed as essential the support of non-Communist governments. American foreign policy was affected by what came to be known as the domino theory. This principle maintained that if one nation in a region fell to the Communists, others in the area would follow. To prevent this from occurring, the United States was willing to participate in limited warfare in isolated parts of the world. Such was the case in Vietnam.

The first official American military advisers arrived in South Vietnam in 1955, after the country was divided at the Geneva Conference. Later that year, Ngo Dinh

General Maxwell Taylor (left), a military adviser to President John F. Kennedy, was one of many advisers who traveled to Saigon to meet with South Vietnam's premier, Ngo Dinh Diem (right).

Diem, the South Vietnamese premier and a determined nationalist (promoter of national independence and a strong central government), called off the elections and proclaimed the South an independent nation.

North Vietnam and China then established and began to outfit and train the Viet Minh, which eventually became known as the Viet Nam Cong San, or Vietcong. The North Vietnamese were determined to unify Vietnam by waging a guerrilla war (a war in which small mobile groupings of fighters employ quick strikes) against Diem and his administration.

U.S. soldiers went into direct combat against the North Vietnamese in 1965. The American public previously had supported wars in which their country had participated.

Above: Antiwar rallies (above) were held on college campuses, in small towns, and in Washington, D.C., during the Vietnam War years. Opposite: In 1965, the United States sent soldiers into direct combat against North Vietnamese forces. Almost fifty-eight thousand soldiers died in Vietnam before total U.S. withdrawal in 1973.

This time, however, increasing numbers of citizens questioned U.S. foreign policy in Vietnam. During the next few years, Americans of all ages, from college students to grandmothers, took to the nation's streets to protest the war.

U.S. involvement in Southeast Asia lasted through a cease-fire in January 1973. Almost fifty-eight thousand American military personnel died in Vietnam.

The war, however, was not yet over. The North initiated a major offensive, and by 1975 controlled all of South Vietnam. On April 30 of that year, North Vietnamese tanks entered Saigon, South Vietnam's capital city. South Vietnam soon surrendered

DENNIS S
BRIAN R ESTES
PETER A DUPERRY
ROBERT E DIEHL
MENDEZ GARCIA
FRANK P EVANGELISTA
MENARD
CARL L RADTKE
JAMES R TAYLOR
WALTERS
JASPER
FREEMAN
EDWARDS

Opposite: The names of all the American casualties of the Vietnam War are engraved on the Vietnam Veterans Memorial in Washington, D.C. Above: In April 1975, North Vietnamese troops entered and occupied Saigon, the capital of South Vietnam.

and, finally, North and South were united as one nation. In 1976, the two became the Socialist Republic of Vietnam. During the decades-long struggle, approximately 3 million Vietnamese soldiers and civilians lost their lives.

The United States committed masses of troops, equipment, and funds to prevent Ho Chi Minh and his followers from ruling Vietnam. In the end, this effort failed. The Vietnam War was the lengthiest conflict in the nation's history, and America's first military defeat.

John F. Kennedy was born in Brookline, Massachusetts, in 1917. After he graduated from Harvard University, he served in the U.S. Navy during World War II. He was elected to the House of Representatives in 1946, and became a U.S. senator six years later. In 1960, Kennedy was selected as the Democratic Party's presidential nominee. In a close election, he beat Republican Richard Nixon and became the thirty-fifth president of the United States.

As early as 1956, Kennedy declared, "Vietnam represents the cornerstone of the Free World in Southeast Asia." Once he became president, Kennedy often spoke of the importance of preserving freedom in South Vietnam, and the need for Americans to regard the conflict between North and South as one small element in a greater battle against what he declared to be a "communist conspiracy" to dominate the world.

In 1961, Kennedy sent his vice president, Lyndon Johnson, on a fact-finding tour of Vietnam; Johnson also conveyed Kennedy's support to Ngo Dinh Diem, the South Vietnamese president. Later that year, Kennedy asked a second representative, General Maxwell Taylor, to travel to Saigon. Taylor's assignment was to determine the extent to which Kennedy should increase financial aid and send military equipment and advisers to assist the South Vietnamese in their battle against the North. Kennedy dispatched large numbers of advisers to South Vietnam. During his administration, the figure rose from two thousand to approximately seventeen thousand. Yet he never sent American soldiers to fight the Communists.

Opposite and above: President John F. Kennedy sent thousands of military advisers to South Vietnam. He advocated the preservation of South Vietnam's freedom and warned against a "communist conspiracy."

On November 22, 1963, Kennedy was assassinated while traveling in a motorcade through downtown Dallas. No one ever will know if he would have committed American combat troops to Vietnam if he had lived. What is clear is that Kennedy's Vietnam policy helped set the stage for U.S. escalation of the war, which took place after his death.

NGO DINH DIEM

DECLARED SOUTH VIETNAM'S INDEPENDENCE

Ngo Dinh Diem, born in 1901 in the Vietnamese city of Hue, hailed from an aristocratic Catholic family. He spent his early career as a civil servant in the French colonial administration and was a dedicated anti-Communist. After World War II, he chose not to participate in the Viet Minh government of Ho Chi Minh. Instead, he went into exile in the United States and Europe.

After the French defeat at Dien Bien Phu in 1954, Diem returned to his homeland and was appointed premier of South Vietnam. An avowed nationalist, he rebuffed the Geneva accord, which temporarily separated Vietnam into North and South. He cancelled the national elections that were scheduled for July 1956 and named himself president of South Vietnam, which he declared an independent nation.

Ngo Dinh Diem (opposite) became the first president of the South Vietnam in 1956. Some Buddhist monks (above) committed suicide by burning themselves to protest the religious policies of Diem's corrupt regime.

Diem's administration was brimming with corruption. Anti-Communists and Diem loyalists were appointed to important government and military posts, rather than those who were more equipped to carry out these jobs. The president refused to introduce land reforms, which would have allowed South Vietnam's peasant class an opportunity to improve their circumstances. He authorized the arrest and torture of anyone suspected of harboring Communist sympathies. Tens of thousands of South Vietnamese were jailed. Most significantly, he oppressed the members of the country's Buddhist majority, who were jailed and executed by the hundreds.

Nonetheless, Diem maintained U.S. support, and continually requested American assistance to fight the Vietcong. That support began to wane in May 1963, when government forces opened fire on demonstrating Buddhists. Diem neither apologized for the tragedy nor acknowledged that his troops had killed the Buddhists. The situation further deteriorated when Buddhist monks attracted international attention by burning themselves to death in protest.

Diem was assassinated in November 1963 during a coup d'état (the overthrow of a government by force) instigated by his generals and reportedly backed by the United States.

LYNDON B. JOHNSON

SENT U.S. TROOPS TO VIETNAM

Lyndon B. Johnson was born on a farm in southwest Texas in 1908. He attended Southwest Texas State Teachers College, and was elected to the U.S. House of Representatives in 1937. He served in the U.S. Navy during World War II and became a U.S. senator in 1948. After an unsuccessful attempt to win the Democratic Party's presidential nomination twelve years later, he became John F. Kennedy's running mate and, with Kennedy's victory, vice president of the United States. Upon Kennedy's assassination, Johnson became the thirty-sixth U.S. president. The following year, he won a landslide victory over his Republican Party opponent, Barry Goldwater.

During his presidency, Johnson spearheaded the passage of wide-ranging legislation that he hoped would wipe out poverty and racial discrimination across the United States. His primary legacy, however, remains his Vietnam policy. Johnson believed that the United States had to fight in Vietnam to prevent North Vietnamese expansion in Southeast Asia. In August 1964, North Vietnamese torpedo boats reportedly attacked a U.S. destroyer in the Gulf of Tonkin. Johnson responded by ordering air strikes over North Vietnam. The U.S. Congress then passed what came to be known as the Gulf of Tonkin Resolution, which stated that "the Congress approves and supports the determination of the President, as Commander in Chief, to take all necessary measures to repel any armed attack against the forces of the United States and to prevent further aggression." The resolution is viewed as the start of full-blown American involvement in the war. Later on, it became controversial for allowing the president too much power.

In 1964, Johnson increased the number of American troops in Vietnam to 25,000. Officially, they still were noncombatants and served as advisers to the South Vietnamese military. The following year, Johnson raised the number to 180,000. At this point, U.S. troops were actively fighting the Communists. Their ranks steadily increased and, by 1968, more than a half-million American soldiers were based in Vietnam.

On March 31, 1968, in the wake of increasing protests against his Vietnam policies, Johnson announced that he would neither seek nor accept the Democratic Party's presidential nomination. He died suddenly of a heart attack at his Texas ranch in 1973.

President Lyndon B. Johnson initiated full-scale U.S. military involvement in Vietnam in 1964. Johnson faced harsh criticism for his Vietnam policies and decided not to run for president in 1968.

HO CHI MINH

Ho Chi Minh was born in 1890 in a small village in central Vietnam. His real name was Nguyen That Thanh. He attended school in the city of Hue, and in 1911 traveled to France to work and study. Legend has it that he showed up at the Versailles Peace Conference, which took place in 1919, at the close of World War I. There, he unsuccessfully tried to hand over to U.S. president Woodrow Wilson a proposal for Vietnam independence from France.

In 1930, Ho founded the Indochinese (Vietnamese) Communist Party in Hong Kong. The party's goals included defeat of the French, formation of an independent government, land reform, education for all, and an eight-hour workday. In 1941, after the Japanese occupied Vietnam, Ho sneaked into his homeland and established the Vietnam Independence League (Viet Minh) to fight the Japanese. After the defeat of the Japanese in 1945, the Viet Minh expected to rule their country, and Ho became president and minister of foreign affairs of the new Democratic Republic of Vietnam. The French, however, reestablished their power and refused to grant Vietnam its independence. Ho was unwilling to allow his country to be ruled by outsiders, and began a guerrilla war against the French.

Opposite: Ho Chi Minh greets French premier Georges Bidault in 1946. Ho won his country's independence from French rule in 1954. Above: Ho remained a revered figure even after his death in 1969.

After the French defeat at Dien Bien Phu in 1954, Ho became president of North Vietnam. Before the end of the decade, he embarked on an armed revolt against the South. The 1960s found Ho in failing health; his role in the fight was primarily that of figurehead, rather than policy maker. He did, however, remain front and center as the North Vietnamese leader. As U.S. president Lyndon Johnson escalated the war, he attempted to deal with Ho and the North Vietnamese through diplomacy. "Old Ho can't turn me down," the U.S. president proclaimed. Nevertheless, the aging revolutionary did. Ho's determination to defeat the South Vietnamese and achieve independence for his country was never more evident than in a simple declaration he made in 1967: "We will never negotiate."

In 1969, Ho died of a heart attack in Hanoi, the capital of North Vietnam. After the war's end, Saigon, which had been capital, was renamed Ho Chi Minh City.

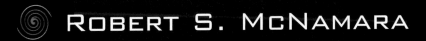

ROBERT S. MCNAMARA

OVERSAW U.S. MILITARY BUILDUP

Robert S. McNamara was born in San Francisco in 1916. He studied economics, philosophy, and business administration at the University of California, Berkeley and Harvard University in Massachusetts, and served in the U.S. Air Force during World War II. After he left the military in 1946, McNamara worked for the Ford Motor Company as a manager of planning and financial analysis. In 1957, he was promoted to company director, and three years later became company president. Later in 1960, McNamara was named secretary of defense by president-elect John F. Kennedy.

Throughout his stretch as defense secretary, McNamara played a key role in influencing and administering U.S. foreign policy—and, in particular, in America's expanding role in Vietnam. He oversaw the increase in American military advisers in South Vietnam, presided over the buildup of combat troops, and supervised an increase in America's overall military strength. In 1961, 2,483,000 Americans were in uniform; during the decade, that number rose to 3,550,000. As defense secretary, McNamara often traveled to Vietnam to personally observe the progress of the war.

McNamara initially was confident that the United States could achieve a victory in Vietnam. No such triumph occurred, however, and he eventually came to doubt that a victory could be won simply by the escalation of the war. Despite U.S. military strategy, Communist presence throughout Vietnam spread. McNamara became hesitant to blindly endorse the growing numbers of fighting soldiers called for by U.S. military commanders. His increasing disappointment over the war effort led him to resign from President Lyndon Johnson's cabinet. On November 29, 1967, Johnson announced that McNamara would leave his post to become president of the World Bank. He did so three months later. His tenure as secretary of defense lasted seven years.

McNamara headed the World Bank until his retirement in 1981. In 1995, he published *In Retrospect: The Tragedy and Lessons of Vietnam*, a memoir in which he offered an overview of his country's Vietnam effort. In the book, McNamara expressed a deep-seated feeling of remorse as he spotlighted the errors that he and his fellow policy makers had made.

As secretary of defense, Robert S. McNamara (left) often traveled to Vietnam to observe U.S. efforts in the war firsthand. As more soldiers were sent to Vietnam, however, McNamara reconsidered his support of the war and resigned from his position in 1967.

WILLIAM C. WESTMORELAND

COMMANDER OF U.S. FORCES

William C. Westmoreland was born in Spartanburg County, South Carolina, in 1914. He graduated from the U.S. Military Academy at West Point, New York, in 1936. He commanded artillery battalions during World War II and an airborne combat team during the Korean War.

By 1964, Westmoreland had risen to the rank of general. That year, he became commander of the U.S. military forces in Vietnam. In 1965, he supervised the first American ground troops in Vietnam, and remained in command during President Lyndon Johnson's escalation of the war. Additionally, Westmoreland was a significant contributor to U.S. military policy. He preferred to employ American combat troops to battle the Communists and reduce the role of the South Vietnamese military. His strategy was to wear away at the enemy by killing them as quickly as possible and not allowing them to replenish their troops. Westmoreland ordered that American combat units head out on "search and destroy" missions to find and eliminate the opposition.

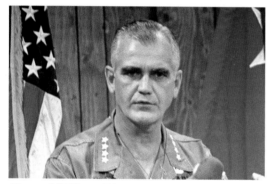

General William Westmoreland advocated a search-and-destroy strategy, which called for U.S. troops to kill North Vietnamese soldiers as quickly as possible to prevent them from replenishing their troops.

The turning point of the war, and of Westmoreland's tenure in Vietnam, began on January 30, 1968. On that date, the Communists launched the Tet Offensive. In this carefully planned attack, the North Vietnamese military and Vietcong struck five large South Vietnamese cities—including the presidential palace and the U.S. embassy in Saigon—as well as more than one hundred district and provincial capitals and countless villages. Newspapers and television networks presented images of the Tet Offensive that shocked the American public. One of the most infamous images featured Nguyen Ngoc Loan, chief of the South Vietnamese National Police, shooting and killing a bound Vietcong prisoner. Another report highlighted the casualties of the attack on the embassy.

Before the Tet Offensive, during the early escalation of the war, journalists rarely doubted Johnson's declarations. Now, however, when the president informed the White House press corps that the Tet Offensive was a "complete failure" on the

As commander of U.S. military forces in Vietnam, Westmoreland supervised American ground troops from the beginning of U.S. involvement until President Johnson relieved him of his duties in 1968.

part of the Communists, he was dismayed to find that journalists no longer accepted such claims without question.

Militarily, the Tet Offensive was in fact a failure, but the media coverage brought home to the American public the brutality of the war. More and more Americans began to question their country's Vietnam policy, and Johnson began to doubt Westmoreland's search-and-destroy strategy. After the Tet Offensive, Westmoreland yet again requested additional ground troops for combat in Vietnam. Instead of receiving them, Westmoreland was relieved of his duties by Johnson.

Westmoreland returned to Washington, D.C., and became the chief of staff of the U.S. Army. He retired in 1972, when it became increasingly apparent that the United States would not be victorious in Vietnam.

Vo Nguyen Giap

Vo Nguyen Giap was born in the Vietnamese province of Quang Binh in 1912. He studied economics at the University of Hanoi and taught history before he joined Ho Chi Minh's Indochinese Communist Party and protested the French presence in his country.

During World War II, Giap joined with Ho Chi Minh and the Viet Minh to resist the Japanese occupation. After the war, their struggle continued, against the French. Giap became the military commander of the Viet Minh, and masterminded the victory against the French at Dien Bien Phu. Instead of simply attacking the French, Giap chose to encircle the opposition and dig a massive central trench. From here, smaller trenches were dug, like the spokes from a wheel, in the direction of the enemy. Before the battle began, Giap was able to position seventy thousand Viet Minh troops—five times the number of the French soldiers—around Dien Bien Phu.

Above: President Johnson realized the United States probably could not win the war after General Vo Nguyen Giap (pictured) launched the Tet Offensive. Opposite: Giap, noted as a brilliant military strategist, remained active in Vietnam's government after the war.

Giap continued as commander-in-chief and chief military strategist of the North Vietnamese and Vietcong throughout the subsequent war. Its turning point came in 1968, when Giap planned and put into action the Tet Offensive, a massive surprise attack launched on the eve of the lunar New Year celebration. In the wake of the Tet Offensive, American television broadcaster Walter Cronkite traveled to Vietnam. Cronkite, the anchor of the *CBS Evening News*, was admired by Americans for his reassuring, fatherly presence and the fairness of his reporting. Even though the Tet Offensive had been put down, Cronkite publicly declared that he no longer believed the United States would win the war. He noted that he was "more certain than ever that the bloody experience in Vietnam is to end in a stalemate." Given Cronkite's stature, this viewpoint alarmed and discouraged President Lyndon Johnson—and further established Giap as a brilliant military strategist and determined, unyielding leader.

Giap remained in charge when North Vietnamese troops marched into Saigon in 1975. By then, he had attained the rank of four-star general. After the war, he served a unified Vietnam as minister of defense and deputy prime minister.

NGUYEN VAN THIEU

Nguyen Van Thieu was born in the southern Vietnamese coastal province of Ninh Thuan in 1923. He attended the National Military Academy in Hue, on Vietnam's central coast. In 1945 and 1946, he briefly joined the Viet Minh, but left because of its Communist orientation. During the first Indochina War, he served in a French-controlled army unit that battled the Viet Minh.

After Ngo Dinh Diem declared South Vietnam an independent nation and named himself president in 1955, Thieu remained in the military and eventually became chief of staff of the South Vietnamese armed forces. He was one of the organizers of the 1963 coup d'état that ousted Diem from power, and was among those responsible for the deposed president's assassination. Soon afterward, he became the country's minister of defense. In 1967, he was elected president of South Vietnam and won reelection four years later.

Thieu maintained power in South Vietnam during the bulk of American involvement—and despite the reality that the South was losing the war. A staunch anti-Communist, he was bitterly opposed to the unification of North and South. He kept appealing to the United States for military and financial aid, which was not forthcoming. By 1974, he was unable to pay the wages of his soldiers, who began to desert. The following year, he revealed that he possessed a letter from President Richard Nixon that assured him of military aid if it appeared that the Communists were winning the war. The only problem was, Nixon was no longer the U.S. president. In April 1975, just before Communist troops occupied Saigon and the

Opposite and above: Nguyen Van Thieu, president of South Vietnam from 1967 to 1975, strongly opposed the reunification of North and South Vietnam and appealed to U.S. president Richard Nixon (above, right) for military and financial aid.

Vietnam War officially ended, Thieu himself resigned from office and left the country.

Thieu first lived in exile in Taiwan and London. Then he settled in the United States, and moved, in 1989, to a suburb of Boston, where he died in 2001.

Richard Nixon was born in Yorba Linda, California, in 1913. He attended Whittier College in California and Duke University Law School in North Carolina, and served in the U.S. Navy during World War II. In 1946, he was elected to the House of Representatives, and became a U.S. Senator in 1950. Next, he served as vice president during the two-term presidency of Republican Dwight Eisenhower, who was first elected in 1952. Nixon then lost the 1960 presidential election to John F. Kennedy, and later the 1962 California gubernatorial race. Despite these defeats, he again was his party's presidential nominee in 1968. This time, Nixon defeated Democrat Hubert H. Humphrey and third-party challenger George Wallace to become the thirty-seventh U.S. president.

While he campaigned for the presidency, Nixon promised to end America's presence in Vietnam. Once elected, he presided over the gradual withdrawal of U.S. troops. In 1969, 550,000 American soldiers were stationed in Vietnam; by late 1972, that number had decreased to 30,000. In what came to be known as the "Vietnamization" of the war, South Vietnamese troops took over the brunt of the fighting.

At the same time, Nixon also authorized the saturation bombing (intense bombing, meant to destroy the entire targeted region) of North Vietnam. He believed that Communist outposts had been established in Laos and Cambodia, neutral nations that bordered Vietnam. For this reason, he approved invasions of Laos and Cambodia that took place during a two-month period that began in April 1970 and involved both U.S. and South Vietnamese forces. Nixon's opponents, however, felt that the invasions only widened the war.

Above: This U.S. Air Force B-52 bomber was shot down in the December 1972 bombing raids on Hanoi ordered by President Richard Nixon. Opposite: Nixon, pictured here with his vice president Spiro Agnew (left), became the thirty-seventh president of the United States in 1968.

During the spring of 1972, a major military offensive by the North Vietnamese jeopardized the survival of the South Vietnamese government. In order to disrupt deliveries of supplies to the Communists, Nixon directed that the U.S. Navy mine the harbor in Haiphong, a North Vietnamese port city. He also stepped up bombing raids over Hanoi.

Meanwhile, the United States and North Vietnam were participating in a series of meetings to negotiate a cease-fire. These summits took place in France and were known as the Paris Peace Talks. In December 1972, when the peace talks slowed down, Nixon authorized a series of nighttime bombing raids on Hanoi and Haiphong. During an eleven-day period, one hundred thousand bombs were dropped on the two cities. At the time, it was the largest bombing raid in history.

In January 1973, the president announced an agreement with the North Vietnamese that ended American participation in the war. The accord also provided for the establishment of a commission to oversee the cease-fire. Nixon declared that the agreement achieved "peace with honor."

Nixon defeated his Democratic Party rival, George McGovern, and won reelection in 1972. His presidency, however, was devastated by the Watergate scandal, which took root during the election campaign when men who represented the Committee to Re-elect the President broke into the headquarters of the Democratic National Committee, located in the Watergate office building in Washington, D.C. Nixon claimed he knew nothing about the burglary, but tape recordings later proved he had tried to divert the inquiry into the incident. On August 8, 1974, he announced that he would resign from office the following day.

Opposite: President Nixon visited U.S. troops in Vietnam in 1969. Above: Because of the Watergate Hotel break-in during the 1972 presidential campaign, Nixon became the only United States president to ever resign from office.

During his last years Nixon lectured and wrote about U.S. foreign policy in an attempt to restore his name. His supporters viewed him as a respected elder statesman, while his critics faulted him for extending the Vietnam War and misrepresenting facts to the American public during the Watergate crisis. In 1994, he died of a massive stroke in New York City.

RON KOVIC

VIETNAM VETERAN TURNED ANTIWAR ACTIVIST

Ron Kovic was born in Ladysmith, a small Wisconsin town, in 1946. As he grew up in Massapequa, a New York City suburb, he came to believe that being a soldier was an exciting and heroic job. After high school graduation, he was inspired by a speech given by a U.S. Marine Corps recruiter. He joined the marines in September 1964.

Kovic was shipped off to fight in Vietnam. Life under fire proved a sobering experience. On one occasion, he accidentally shot a young American corporal. He tried to confess to his superiors, and was disturbed that they chose to ignore the incident. Another time, his platoon was ordered to kill the reportedly armed inhabitants of a village. Afterwards, as he helped count the dead, he was appalled to discover that the deceased were unarmed women, children, and elderly men. Finally, on January 20, 1968, Kovic was shot in the shoulder while in combat. His spinal cord was shattered, and he was paralyzed from the chest down.

Kovic expected to return home to a hero's welcome. Instead, he found an America deeply divided over the war effort. He was all but forgotten, and was confined to gloomy New York City veterans' hospitals. Kovic was depressed and angry, but his rage eventually turned to political activism. This former gung-ho recruit emerged as an eloquent antiwar activist. He began to attend antiwar rallies and speak about his Vietnam experiences to high school students.

Kovic protested the war at the Republican National Convention in August 1972. After he attempted to interrupt Richard Nixon's acceptance speech, he was interviewed by CBS news correspondent Roger Mudd. "I'm a Vietnam veteran," he declared. "I gave America my all, and the leaders of this government threw me and others away to rot in their VA hospitals. What's happening in Vietnam is a crime against humanity."

Four years later, Kovic made a return appearance during the presidential race. This time, however he addressed the Democratic National Convention. Also in 1976, he published *Born on the Fourth of July*, one of the era's enduring memoirs, in which he traced his experiences before, during, and after Vietnam. *Born on the Fourth of July* was made into a film in 1989, with Tom Cruise starring as Kovic.

Kovic eventually settled in Redondo Beach, California. He continues to speak out about the perils of war and to assist other Vietnam veterans.

Ron Kovic, a former U.S. Marine who served in Vietnam, became a prominent activist against the war after he returned home paralyzed from the chest down.

WILLIAM CALLEY

CONVICTED OF THE MY LAI MASSACRE

William Calley was born in 1945, and grew up in Florida. He graduated from Miami Edison Senior High School and attended Palm Beach Junior College.

In July 1966, Calley dropped out of school and joined the U.S. Army. After he became a clerk-typist, he attended Officer Candidates School and spent six months training as a junior officer. He was given the rank of lieutenant and in November 1967 was dispatched to Vietnam.

In March 1968, Calley and his platoon entered My Lai, a small South Vietnamese village that allegedly was teeming with Vietcong. He ordered his troops to shoot all of the village's inhabitants. They killed between one hundred and five hundred unarmed women, children, and elderly men. One of Calley's soldiers eventually told the story of My Lai to Ron Ridenhour, a Vietnam veteran. Ridenhour investigated the account and presented his findings to government and military officials. In late 1969, Life magazine published photos of the massacre, snapped by an army photographer.

In 1971, Calley went on trial for his role in the massacre. One juror declared that the jury "had labored long and hard to find some way, some evidence, some flaw in the testimony so we could find Lt. Calley innocent." Nonetheless, he was found guilty of the murder of "at least 22" of the My Lai villagers, and sentenced to life in prison. No one else ever was charged with crimes connected to the massacre.

Opposite: Lt. William Calley emerges from a courthouse during his 1971 trial for his role in the My Lai massacre. Above: These women were among the few survivors of the My Lai massacre, in which Calley ordered his troops to shoot all of the inhabitants of the small South Vietnamese village.

Some viewed Calley as a scapegoat for the inability of the U.S. Army to infuse its troops with self-control. Others felt he was a war criminal.

Despite the seriousness of the crime and Calley's conviction, President Richard Nixon set aside his prison sentence and ordered that he be placed under house arrest. He was pardoned in 1974. Calley settled in Columbus, Georgia. He married in 1975, and became the manager of a jewelry store owned by his father-in-law.

DANIEL ELLSBERG

GAVE CLASSIFIED MILITARY DOCUMENTS TO THE MEDIA

Daniel Ellsberg was born in Detroit in 1931. He attended Harvard University, where he earned a Ph.D. in economics, and served in the U.S. Marines Corps. He then was hired as an economic analyst by the Rand Corporation, a nonprofit institution that analyzes issues that relate to public welfare and U.S. security. His assignment was to explore problems that might arise during the fighting of a nuclear war.

In 1964, Ellsberg began to work at the Pentagon as a special assistant in charge of coordinating Vietnam strategy. The following year, he was dispatched to South Vietnam in the employ of the U.S. State Department, on the staff of the special assistant to U.S. ambassador Henry Cabot Lodge. While in Vietnam, Ellsberg traveled throughout the country to observe the progress of the war. Occasionally, he found himself in combat situations. After he spent two years in Vietnam, he continued to work for the federal government and the Rand Corporation.

Anitwar advocate Daniel Ellsberg has lectured and written books about his experiences, both in Vietnam and in the United States, as a Pentagon strategist during the Vietnam War.

While employed at the Pentagon and State Department, Ellsberg had access to classified documents that contained top-secret information regarding America's Vietnam policies. Their content, coupled with his firsthand observations in Vietnam, made him realize that, as he declared in 1999, "our efforts had been illegitimate. . . . I saw the war as having been wrong from the start. And I was determined to try to help end it as quickly as possible."

Ellsberg photocopied the secret documents, which came to be known as the Pentagon Papers. They were leaked to the media, and were published in the *New York Times* in June 1971. The seven-thousand-page manuscript spotlights U.S. strategy in Vietnam between 1945 and 1968. It contains evidence relating to secrecy among the branches of the federal government, lies put forth by U.S. officials to the public, and falsehoods on the part of U.S. presidents Truman, Eisenhower, Kennedy, and Johnson. One example occurred in August 1964. North Vietnamese torpedo boats reportedly attacked a U.S. destroyer in the Gulf of Tonkin in northeastern Vietnam, which resulted in U.S. escalation of the war. According to the Pentagon Papers, the attack may not have occurred. If it did, it may have been incited because the destroyer had been on a secret mission, and was inside North Vietnamese territorial waters.

Ellsberg spoke to the press after his arrest for giving the New York Times *the Pentagon Papers, top-secret documents that detailed the America's Vietnam policies, in June 1971.*

The publishing of the Pentagon Papers further eroded the already diminishing public support for the Vietnam War. Ellsberg, meanwhile, was arrested for espionage, theft, and conspiracy, but all charges against him were dismissed. He was viewed as a traitor by some and a hero and patriot by others.

Since then, Ellsberg has written books and articles, and lectured about his Vietnam-era experiences. In 2002, he published *Secrets: A Memoir of Vietnam and the Pentagon Papers*.

ABBIE HOFFMAN

Abbie Hoffman was born in Wooster, Massachusetts, in 1936, and attended Brandeis University in Waltham, Massachusetts, and the University of California, Berkeley. He then was employed as a psychologist at a Massachusetts state hospital. In the early 1960s, he worked as a civil rights organizer in Mississippi.

As President Lyndon Johnson began to send combat troops to Vietnam, Hoffman became one of the antiwar movement's high-profile activists. He had a keen understanding of the manner in which the media manipulated public opinion. His strategy was to attract attention by satirizing his cultural and political opponents, the leaders of the American establishment. For example, in 1967, he and several others tossed dollar bills from the New York Stock Exchange visitors' gallery onto the exchange floor. During another demonstration, he directed thousands of antiwar protesters in a comic effort to merge their psychic energy and levitate the Pentagon.

Hoffman and fellow activist Jerry Rubin cofounded the Youth International Party (YIP, or Yippies), a mock political party. The Yippies were one of the groups that organized a war protest at the 1968 Democratic National Convention in Chicago; they presented as their presidential candidate Pigasus, a hog. During the convention, the Chicago police clubbed and used tear gas on the protesters. Afterwards, Hoffman and other rally organizers were indicted and accused of scheming to incite a riot. They became known as the Chicago 7, and their trial made national headlines. The defendants were found innocent of some charges and guilty of others. Their convictions eventually were overturned by a court of appeals because of, among other reasons, the original trial judge's "deprecatory and antagonistic attitude toward the defense."

In 1973, Hoffman was arrested for allegedly attempting to sell cocaine. The following year, he took the name Barry Freed and went into hiding. For the next six years, he lived in upstate New York and worked as an environmental activist. He then gave himself up to the authorities and, after he served a short prison sentence, continued his political activism. In 1987, he was arrested while demonstrating against Central Intelligence Agency (CIA) recruiters at the University of Massachusetts.

Hoffman died in 1989 at his home in New Hope, Pennsylvania. His death was declared a suicide.

Abbie Hoffman was one of the most high-profile antiwar activists of the Vietnam War era. One of the Chicago 7, Hoffman organized many protests, including one at the 1968 Democratic National Convention.

HENRY KISSINGER

Henry Kissinger was born in Fuerth, Germany, in 1923. He immigrated to the United States in 1938, and became a U.S. citizen five years later. After he served in the U.S. Army, he attended Harvard University. He joined the Harvard faculty in 1954, and was affiliated with the university's Center for International Affairs and the Department of Government.

After Richard Nixon was elected president in 1968, he named Kissinger his national security adviser. Kissinger was a key player in devising America's foreign policy during the Nixon presidency and in conducting peace negotiations with the North Vietnamese. For his efforts in brokering the cease-fire in Vietnam, he was awarded the Nobel Peace Prize in 1973. He shared the honor with Le Duc Tho, his North Vietnamese counterpart. Kissinger also became secretary of state in 1973 and served, under Nixon and his successor, Gerald Ford, until 1977.

Henry Kissinger (opposite) negotiated the Vietnam cease-fire agreement. A representative for Vietnamese president Thieu, Nixon, and Kissinger (above, left to right) finalized the agreement in November 1972.

Kissinger, however, remains a controversial figure. His supporters claim that his dealings not only with North Vietnam but with Communist China, the Soviet Union, Israel, and Egypt promoted peaceful international relations. During the Watergate scandal, and the downfall of Nixon, Kissinger kept America's foreign policy on course. His detractors state that Kissinger, in his international dealings, often ignored human rights when fighting communism. With regard to the Vietnam War, they offer as evidence his connection to the bombing of Cambodia, a neutral nation. In 1973, it was revealed that, despite Nixon's statements to the contrary, the United States had shelled Communist targets in Cambodia in 1969 and during the first months of 1970. Not only was this strategy illegal, but it led to the 1975 overthrow of the Cambodian government by Pol Pot, a tyrant whose policies resulted in the deaths of 2 million Cambodians.

Since his government service, Kissinger has lectured, written, and commented on American foreign policy on television news programs. In 2002, President George W. Bush announced that Kissinger would supervise a government inquiry into the events that surrounded the September 11, 2001, terrorist attacks against the United States. Almost immediately, Kissinger left the post because of a conflict of interest with his private consulting firm, Kissinger Associates.

JOHN MCCAIN

HANOI HILTON PRISONER WHO BECAME A U.S. SENATOR

John McCain's father and grandfather were U.S. Navy admirals. He was born in a naval hospital in the Panama Canal Zone in 1936. Upon graduation from the U.S. Naval Academy in 1958, he attended flight training school and became a navy aviator.

Lieutenant Commander McCain volunteered for combat duty in Vietnam. He was just about to take off on a 1967 bombing run over North Vietnam from the USS *Forrestal*, an aircraft carrier, when a missile from another plane accidentally was fired. The rocket hit the fuel tank of McCain's plane, which burst into flames. He narrowly escaped, but the explosions and fires that followed resulted in the loss of more than twenty naval aircraft, hundreds of injuries, and 134 casualties.

Above: In 2000, John McCain visited the "Hanoi Hilton" jail, where he spent nearly six years as a POW. Opposite: McCain (bottom right) made twenty-three bombing missions as a combat pilot in Vietnam before he was shot down.

Despite the mishap, McCain was determined to continue as a combat pilot and was transferred to the USS *Oriskany*. Less than three months later, he set off on his twenty-third bombing mission. His target was a power plant in Hanoi. During the mission, McCain's A-4 Skyhawk bomber was hit by a surface-to-air missile. Its right wing was shot off, and the bomber began to spin toward Earth. As McCain ejected from the plane, both his arms and his right leg were broken, and he lost consciousness. He landed in a lake, from which he was pulled by an irate crowd of North Vietnamese who beat him repeatedly. Then McCain was put in a truck and taken to the infamous prison, ironically named "Hanoi Hilton," which housed American prisoners of war (POWs).

McCain's captors denied him medical treatment; he survived because of the care of his fellow prisoners. For the next five and a half years, he remained a POW. He often was beaten and tortured, and spent two years in solitary confinement. Despite his ill-treatment, he refused offers to be released before his fellow POWs who had been held longer. This would violate the military code of conduct, and McCain was concerned that the Communists would use this special treatment for propaganda purposes.

McCain became one of the almost six hundred POWs released by North Vietnam in 1973. After he underwent physical rehabilitation, he continued his naval career and retired in 1981. He immediately entered politics, and was elected to the House of Representatives in 1982. He became a U.S. senator in 1986 as a representative for state of Arizona, and unsuccessfully ran for president in 2000.

1859	The French capture Saigon, a major city in the southern part of Vietnam.
1862	The French occupy Cochin China, the area of Southeast Asia that would eventually become South Vietnam.
September 22, 1940	Japanese troops invade Vietnam.
1941	Ho Chi Minh establishes the Viet Minh, a guerrilla army, to battle the Japanese.
September 2, 1945	The Japanese surrender, and Ho Chi Minh reads the Vietnamese Declaration of Independence to 500,000 Vietnamese in Hanoi.
1945–46	The French reestablish control in the southern part of Vietnam, and threaten to take over the North from the Viet Minh.
March 13–May 7, 1954	The Viet Minh attack Dien Bien Phu, a French-controlled military outpost. The French eventually surrender, and withdraw from Vietnam.
May 8–July 29, 1954	Vietnam temporarily is divided into North and South at the Geneva Conference. The Communists under Ho Chi Minh will rule the North, while the South will be non-Communist. National elections, which will unify the country, are scheduled for July 1956.
January 1955	The United States begins to send military advisers to South Vietnam.
October 26, 1955	South Vietnamese president Ngo Dinh Diem calls off national elections, and proclaims South Vietnam an independent nation.
1956	The Viet Nam Cong (or Vietcong) is established as a guerrilla army to battle Diem. They are trained and supported by North Vietnam.
December 1960	More than 3,200 American military advisers are posted in Vietnam.
1963	The number of American military advisers reaches 16,700.
May–June, 1963	South Vietnamese troops kill nine Buddhists protesting the Diem regime. The first of six Buddhist monks burns himself to death in further protest.
November 1, 1963	Diem is ousted from office and killed by South Vietnamese military officers.
August 1964	A North Vietnamese torpedo boat allegedly attacks a U.S. destroyer in the Gulf of Tonkin. The U.S. Congress passes the Gulf of Tonkin Resolution.

Vietnamese women and children huddled together as U.S. soldiers entered their village in 1967. By that time, there were more than 350,000 U.S. troops in Vietnam.

February, 1965	The United States begins to bomb North Vietnam.
March, 1965	The first 3,500 American combat troops arrive in Vietnam. By the end of the year, they will number 180,000.
1966	The number of U.S. troops in Vietnam reaches 350,000. The Vietcong steps up its guerrilla war.
September 3, 1967	Nguyen Van Thieu becomes president of South Vietnam.
January 30, 1968	The North Vietnamese launch the Tet Offensive.
1969	The Paris Peace Talks begin.
1969	President Richard Nixon reveals that U.S. combat troops will be with drawn slowly, to be replaced by their South Vietnamese counterparts. His strategy is known as "Vietnamization."
Late 1969/early 1970	The United States secretly shells targets in Cambodia.
April, 1970	U.S. and South Vietnamese forces invade Laos and Cambodia.
June 13, 1971	Excerpts of the Pentagon Papers begin to appear in the U.S. media.
December, 1972	The Paris Peace Talks waver, and Nixon authorizes a series of substantial nighttime bombing raids on Hanoi and Haiphong—the largest in history to date.
August 15, 1973	The United States halts its bombing of North Vietnam.
April 30, 1975	North Vietnamese troops occupy Saigon, and the Vietnam War officially ends.
July 2, 1976	North and South Vietnam formally become the unified Socialist Republic of Vietnam.

For Further Information

Books

Dunn, John M., *A History of U.S. Involvement: The Vietnam War*. San Diego: Lucent Books, 2001.

Gavin, Philip, *The Fall of Vietnam*. San Diego, Lucent Books, 2003.

Gay, Kathlyn, and Martin K. Gay, *Vietnam War*. New York: Twenty-First Century Books, 1996.

Haugen, David M., *The Vietnam War: Primary Sources*. San Diego: Lucent Books, 2002.

Kent, Deborah, *The Vietnam War: "What Are We Fighting For?"* Hillside, NJ: Enslow, 1994.

Websites

Vietnam Online Website produced for the Public Broadcasting System (PBS).
http://www.pbs.org/wgbh/amex/vietnam
This website accompanies *Vietnam: A Television History*, a television series produced by WGBH Boston.

Vietnam War Internet Project
www.vwip.org
A comprehensive site that features articles, memoirs, images, and primary source documents.

ABOUT THE AUTHOR

Rob Edelman is a writer who lives with his wife, Audrey Kupferberg, in Amsterdam, New York. He has authored several books on baseball and movie and television personalities, and teaches film history at the University at Albany. He enjoys watching old movies and attending baseball games.

INDEX